Note: Have the child name the pictures, listening to the short sound of the letter **a**, then complete the page.

A 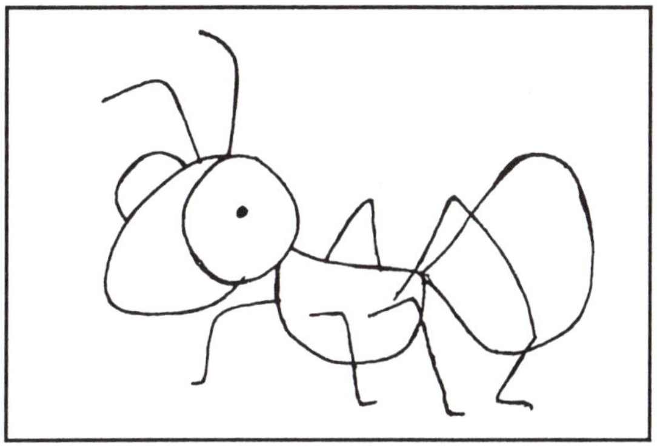   a

A

a

hat   bat

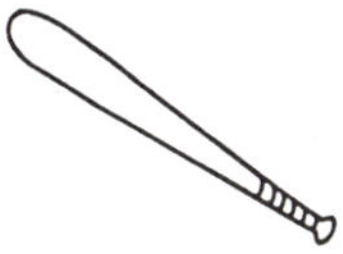

cat   rat

mat   ant

1

Start at 1.
Connect the dots.

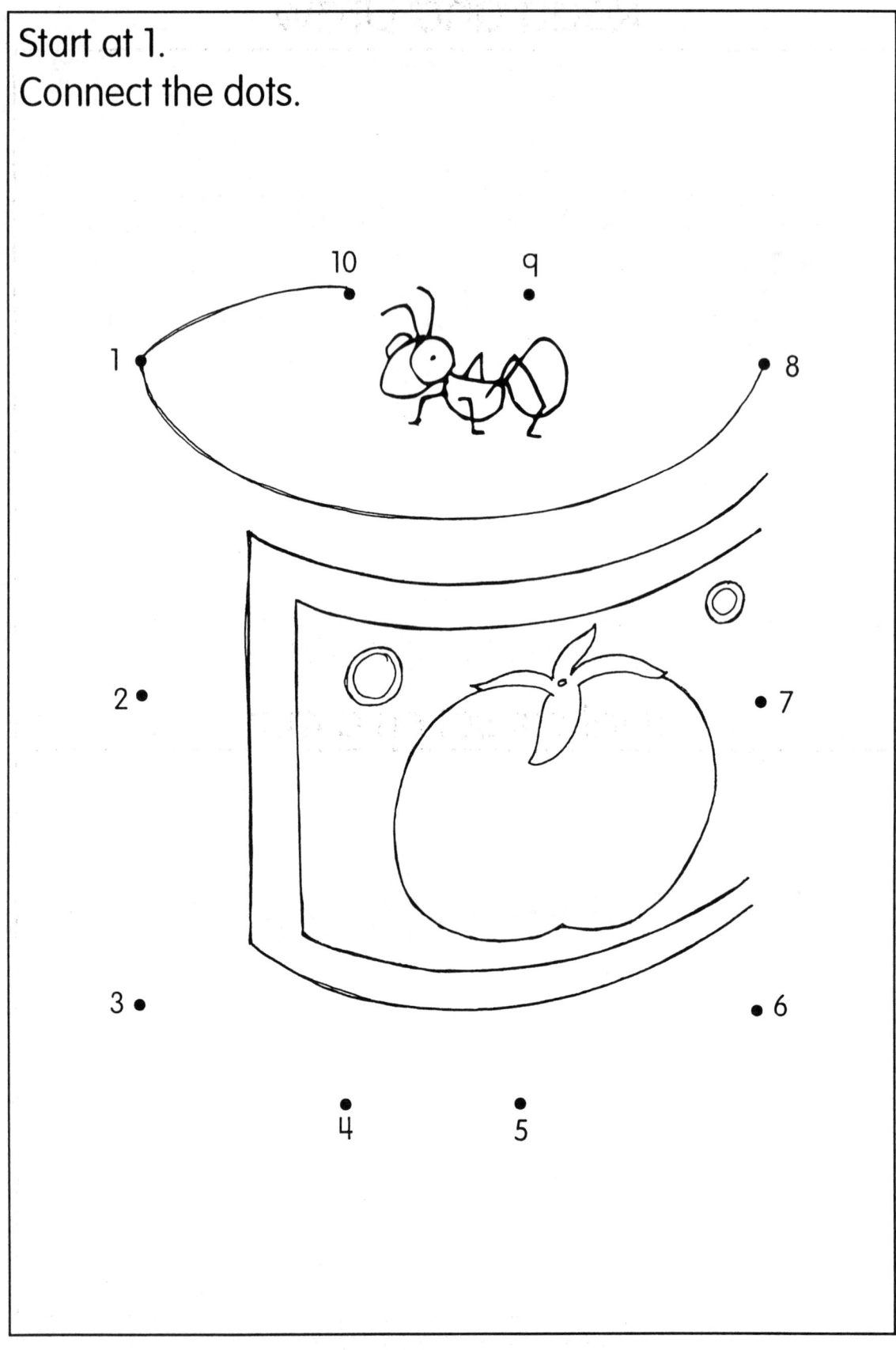

An _____ is on the _____.

Name _____

Read and Draw

a fat cat sat on a mat

a rat had a hat

Note: Have the child name the pictures, listening to the short sound of the letter **e**, then complete the page.

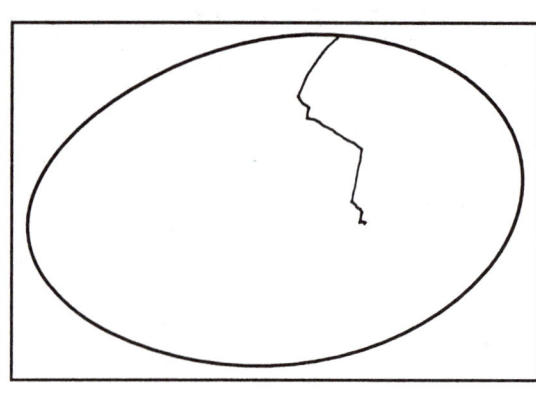

E   e

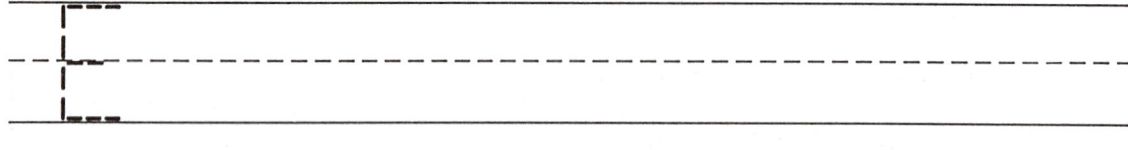

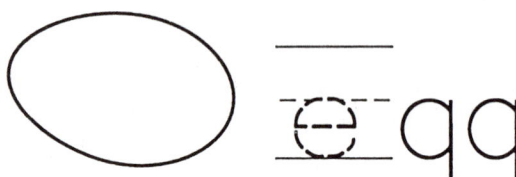 egg    __lf

 h__n   10 t__n

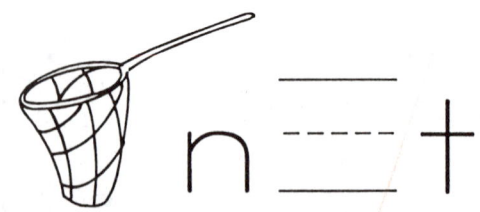 n__t   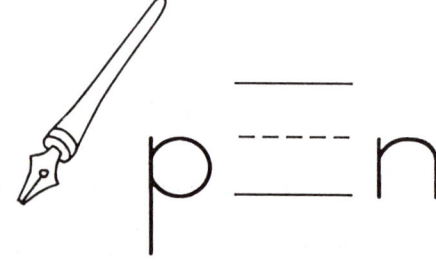 p__n

4

Note: Have the child name the pictures, listening to the short sound of the letter **i**, then complete the page.

7

Start at 1.
Connect the dots.

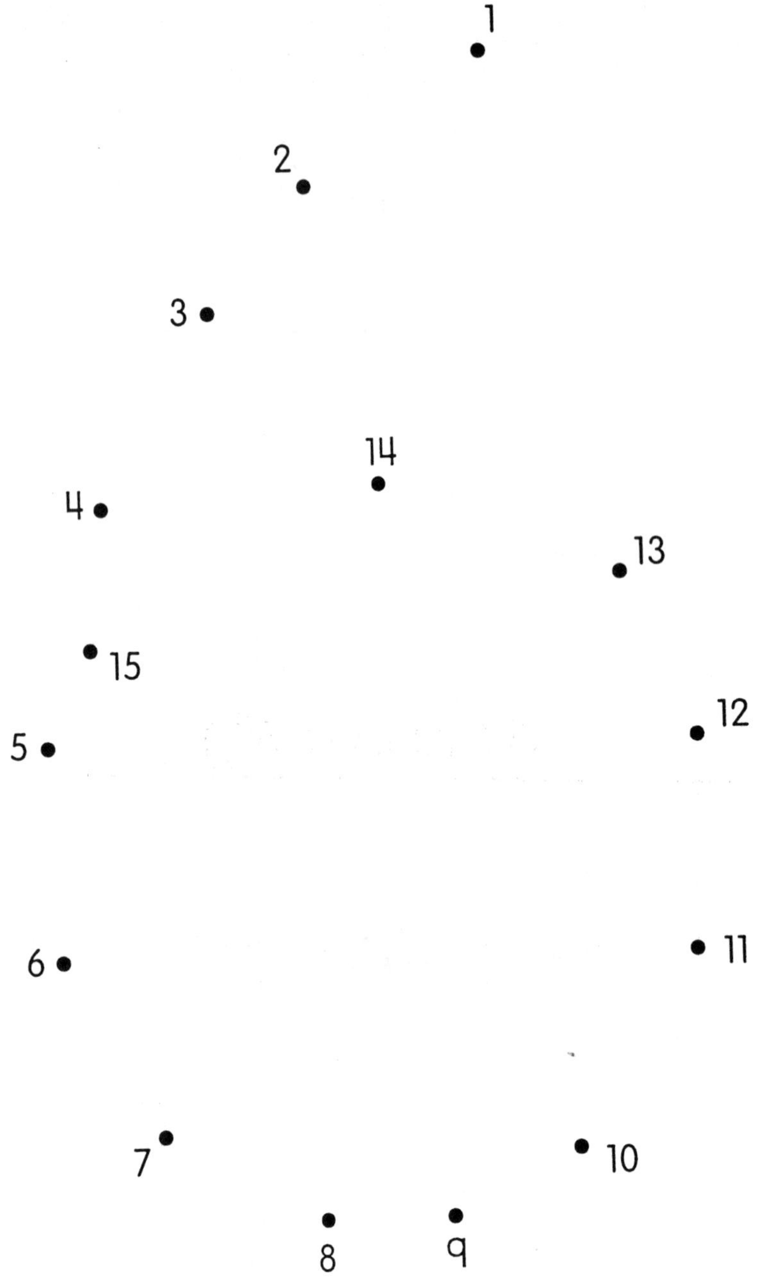

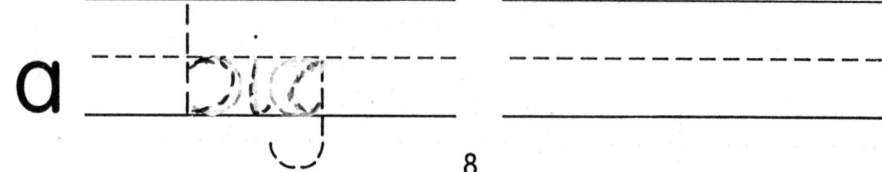

Name _____

Read and Draw

a pig in a wig

six big pigs

Name _____

Note: Have the child name the pictures, listening to the short sound of the letter **o**, then complete the page.

O   o

○- -

- -
○- -

_o_ x   b _o_ x

d _o_ g   t _o_ p

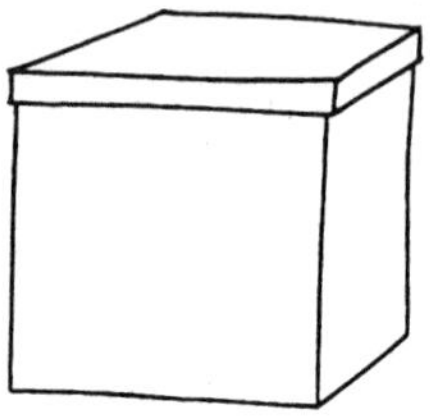

_o_ tter   f _o_ x

10

Start at 1.
Connect the dots.

a _____ in a _____

Read and Draw

a dog on a log

a top in a box

Note: Have the child name the pictures, listening to the short sound of the letter **u**, then complete the page.

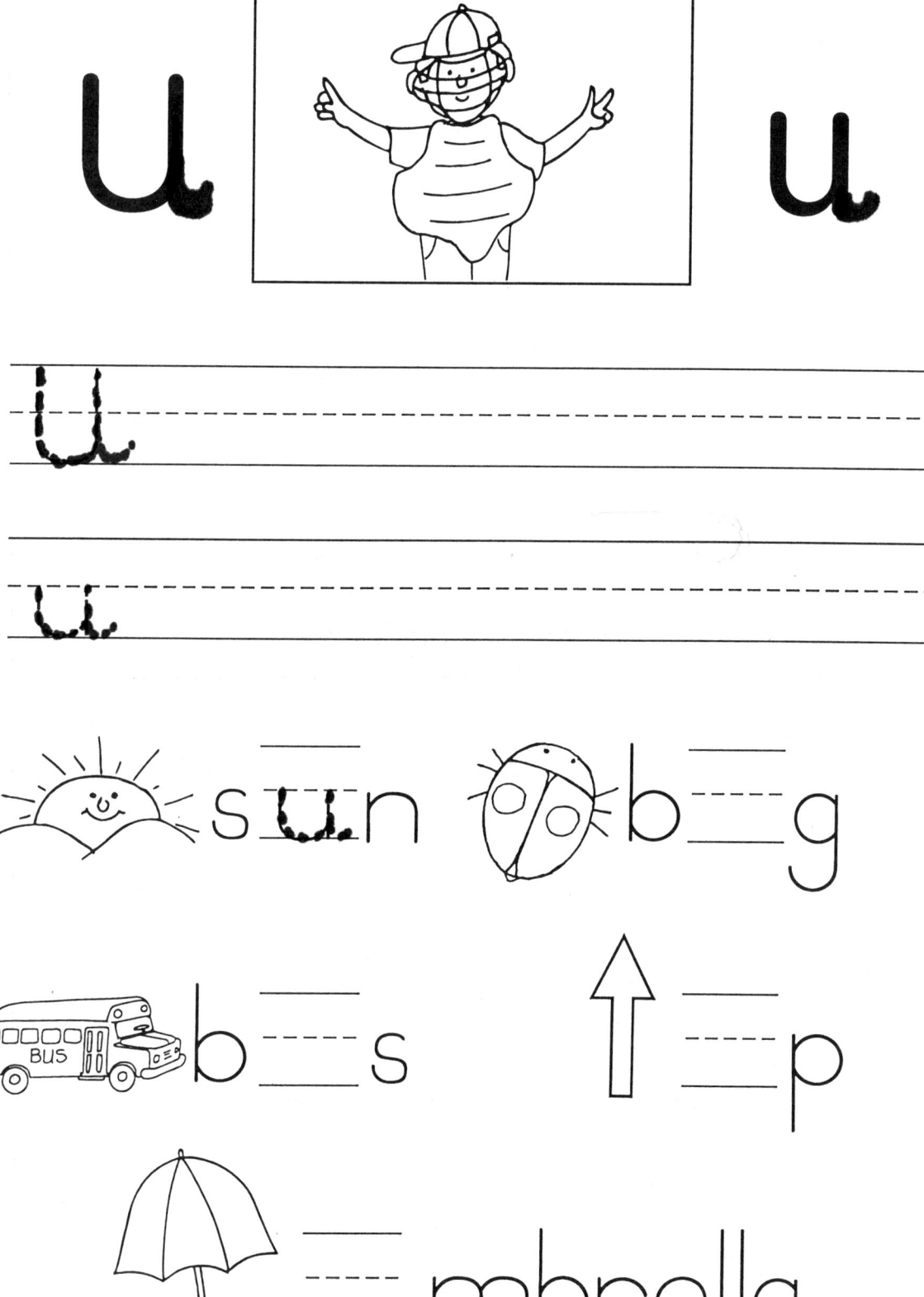

Start at 1.
Connect the dots.

a _____ is on a _____

Read and Draw

a nut is in a cup

a pup is in the mud

a e i o u

Match the vowel sounds.

Read.
Match.

hot dog

cub hug

hot sun

pig pen

egg box

ant hill

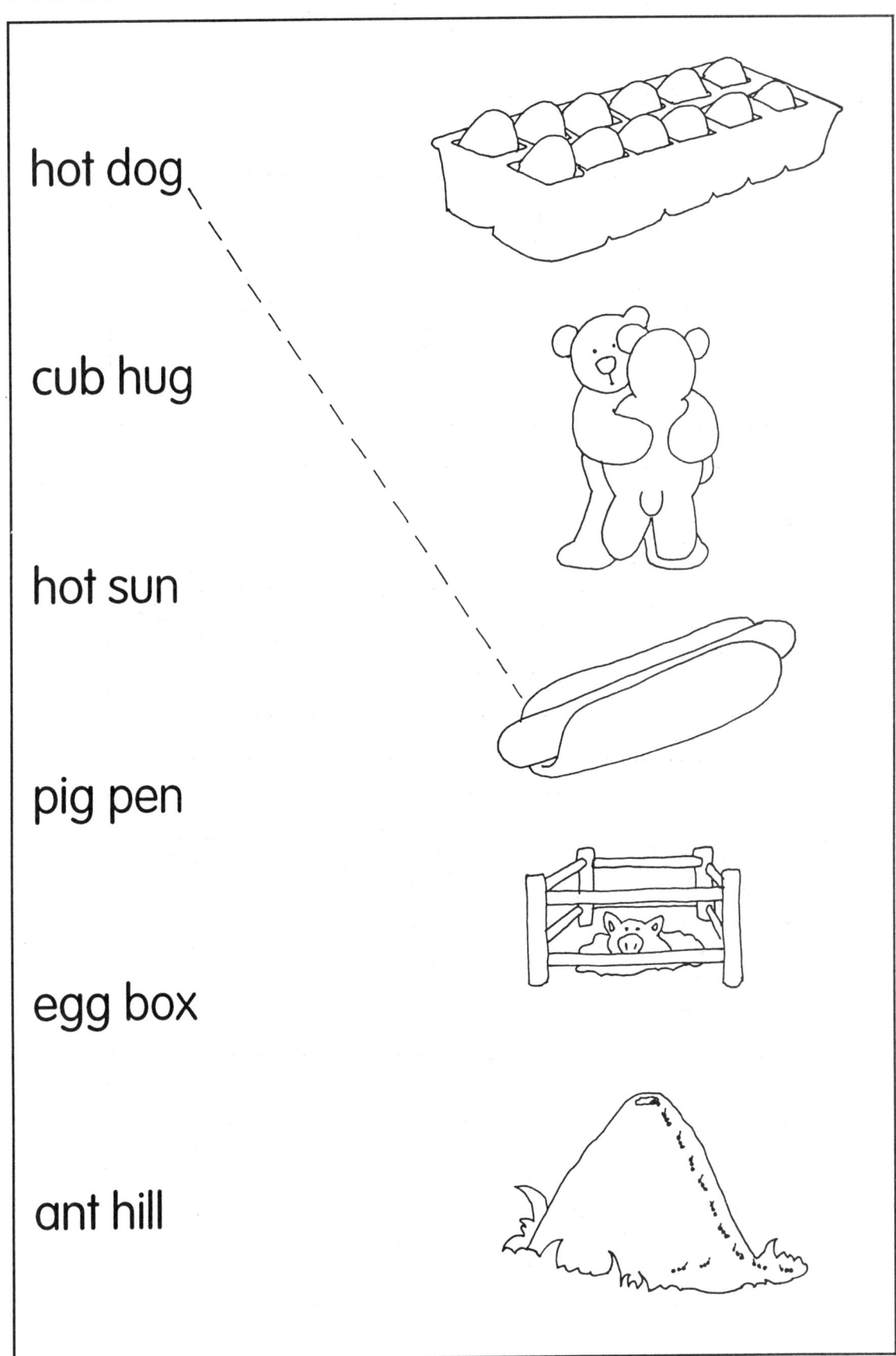

Name _____

Read and Draw

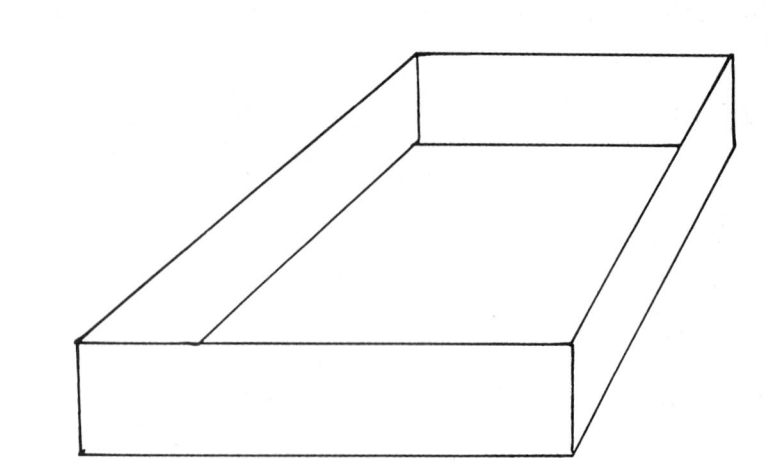

a big egg in the red box

a black hat on the man

a fat pig in the pen

Follow the words that rhyme with <u>cat</u> to get to the <u>rat</u>.

cub	pot	cat	ten
bat	sat	hat	cot
fat	let	can	hot
mat	pat	rat	cut

Read.
Match.

a rat on a hill

an egg in a pan

a hat on a man

a dog on a log

a bat in a net

a dog in a bed

20

Read.
Match.

The cat is fat.

The dog can run.

The fox is red.

The bed is big.

The man is hot.

The ant sat.

This
the

The Pond

This is a big pond.

A log is in the pond.

A frog is on the log.

Jump, frog, jump.

I read this story to_____.

Draw:

| frog | log |

Fill in:

The pond is _____ .

A _____ is in the pond.

A _____ is on the log.

| the bath |

Pat and Sam

Sam digs in the mud.

Sam is a mess.

Pat is mad!

"Sam must get a bath."

I read this story to_____.

Match:

Pat

mud

bath

Sam

Sam digs in _____.

Pat is _____.

Sam must get a _____.

| What the | What is in the box?

Bob had a box.
The box had a lid.
Bob set the box on the step.
What is in the box?

"Get the box, Jan."

Jan gets the box.

She can not see in it.

What is in the box?

Pick What

"Pick up the lid, Jan."

What is in the box?

for
toy

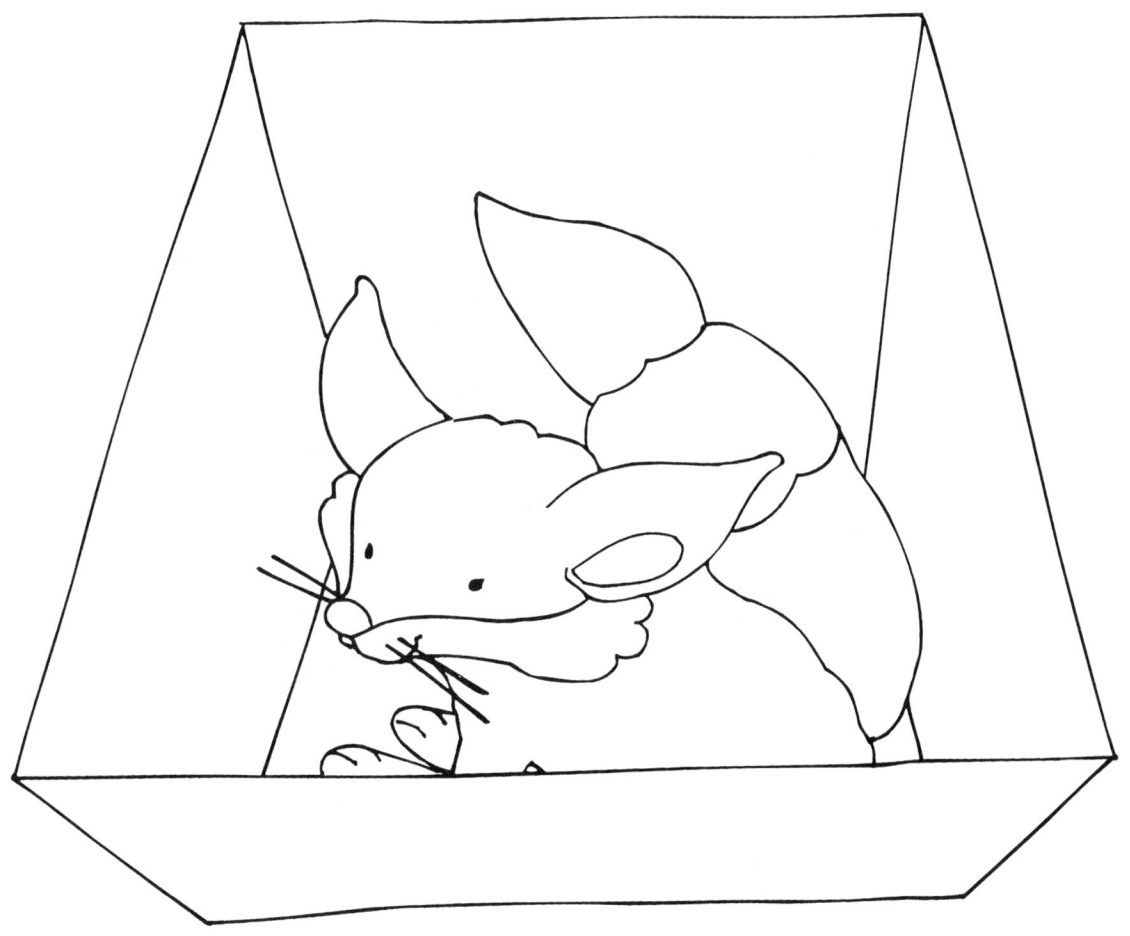

A fox is in the box.

It is a toy fox.

The toy fox is for Jan.

I read this story to_____.

Match:

Jan

fox

step

box

Bob

A _____ is in the box.

It is for _____.

_____ got the toy fox for Jan.

30

Answer Key

Please take time to go over the work your child has completed. Ask your child to explain what he/she has done. Praise both success and effort. If mistakes have been made, explain what the answer should have been and how to find it. Let your child know that mistakes are a part of learning. The time you spend with your child helps let him/her know you feel learning is important.

page 1

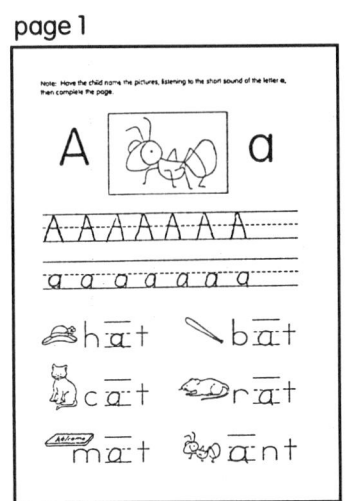

page 2

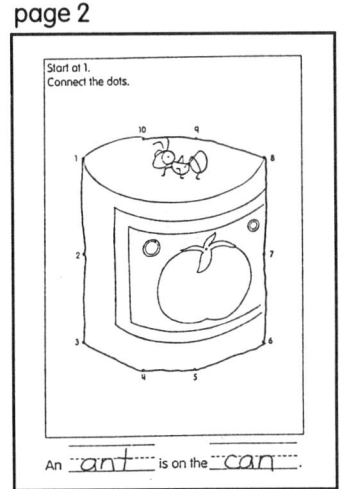

page 3

page 4

page 5

page 6

page 7

page 8

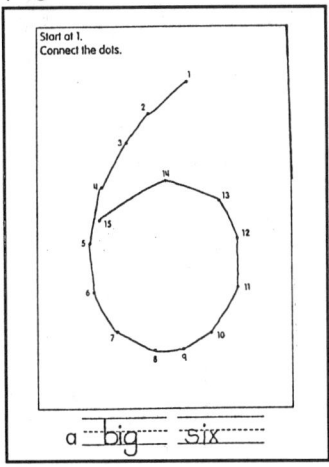

page 9

page 10

page 11

page 12
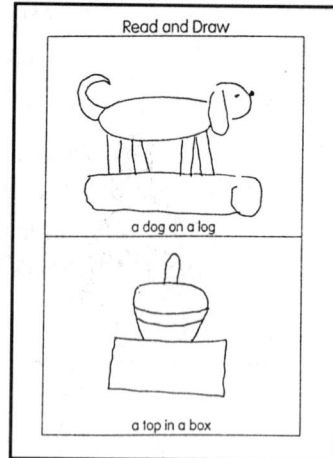

page 13

page 14

page 15

page 16
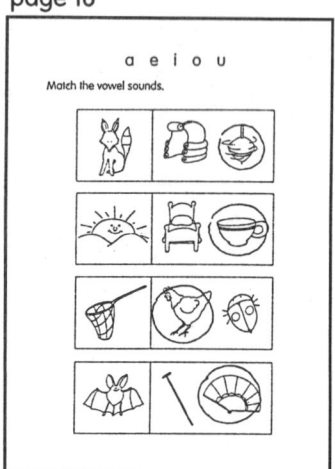

page 17
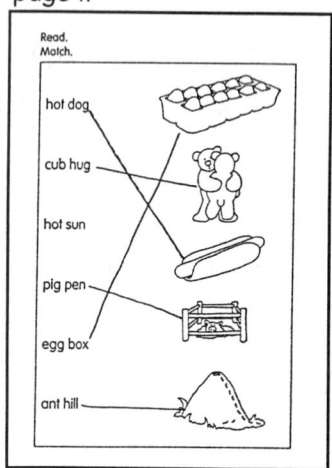

page 18

page 19
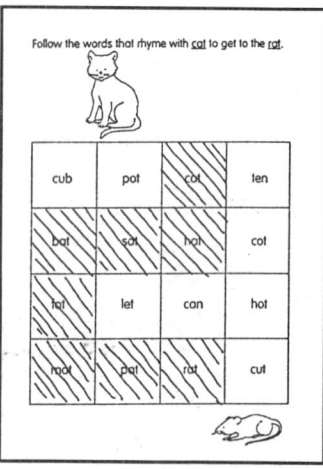

page 20

page 21